GALE
CENGAGE Learning

Novels for Students, Volume 7

Staff

Series Editor: Deborah A. Stanley.

Contributing Editors: Sara L. Constantakis, Catherine L. Goldstein, Motoko Fujishiro Huthwaite, Arlene M. Johnson, Erin White.

Editorial Technical Specialist: Karen Uchic.

Managing Editor: Joyce Nakamura.

Research: Victoria B. Cariappa, *Research Team Manager*. Andy Malonis, *Research Specialist*. Tamara C. Nott, Tracie A. Richardson, and Cheryl L. Warnock, *Research Associates*. Jeffrey Daniels, *Research Assistant*.

Permissions: Susan M. Trosky, *Permissions Manager*. Maria L. Franklin, *Permissions Specialist*. Sarah Chesney, *Permissions Associate*.

Production: Mary Beth Trimper, *Production Director*. Evi Seoud, *Assistant Production*

Manager. Cindy Range, *Production Assistant*.

Graphic Services: Randy Bassett, *Image Database Supervisor*. Robert Duncan and Michael Logusz, *Imaging Specialists*. Pamela A. Reed, *Photography Coordinator*. Gary Leach, *Macintosh Artist*.

Product Design: Cynthia Baldwin, *Product Design Manager*. Cover Design: Michelle DiMercurio, *Art Director*. Page Design: Pamela A. E. Galbreath, *Senior Art Director*.

Copyright Notice

of this work have added value to the underlying factual material herein through one or more of the following: unique and original selection, coordination, expression, arrangement, and classification of the information. All rights to this publication will be vigorously defended.

ISBN 0-7876-3826-9
ISSN 1094-3552

Printed in the United States of America.
10 9 8 7 6 5 4 3 2 1

The Hitchhiker's Guide to the Galaxy

Douglas Adams 1979

Introduction

When *The Hitchhiker's Guide to the Galaxy* was first broadcast as a 12-part radio series on the British Broadcasting System in 1978, it was successful. No one could have guessed, though, that it would mushroom into a multimedia phenomenon that would encompass five novels, a television series, a stage production, and, more than twenty years later, dozens of websites created by devotees who could not get enough of its bizarre universe. Douglas Adams's novel based on the series, *The*

Hitchhiker's Guide to the Galaxy concerns the exploits of Arthur Dent, an average British citizen who gets caught up in a myriad of space adventures when his house, and then the Earth, is demolished. With no planet to call home, he is left to hitchhike through space with his friend Ford Prefect, whom he thought was an out-of-work actor, but who is really a researcher for the intergalactic guidebook named in the title. Adams's book is one in which literally anything can happen, with the only rule being that what comes next will probably be the last thing the reader would expect and is bound to be amusing.

Author Biography

Douglas Adams was born in 1952, in Cambridge, England. He attended school at John's College in Cambridge, where he began his career writing comedy sketches, and received his master of arts degree. In 1978 he began writing radio scripts for the British Broadcasting System. One of the series he created was *The Hitchhiker's Guide to the Galaxy*, which he produced and wrote. The series ran in twelve installments in 1978. For two years he was a script editor and writer for the world-renowned, long-running *Dr. Who* television show.

Because of the popularity *The Hitchhiker's Guide* had on radio, a publishing house approached Adams to turn the series into a novel—up to that point, he had never even considered writing a novel. The book sold an astounding 100,000 copies in the first month of its publication in 1979. *The Hitchhiker's Guide to the Galaxy* has inspired four sequels—*The Restaurant at the End of the Universe; Life, The Universe and Everything; So Long, and Thanks for All the Fish;* and *Mostly Harmless*. Collectively, more than fourteen million copies of the five books have been sold. Because of the huge popularity of *The Hitchhiker's Guide to the Galaxy*, it has also been adapted to a stage play, a television series, and a computer game, and the scripts from the original radio series have been published.

Douglas Adams has also written another science-fiction series that is similar in style to *The Hitchhiker's Guide* books. In *Dirk Gently's Holistic Detective Agency* (1987) and *The Long Dark Tea-Time of the Soul* (1988), Dirk Gently, a time-hopping detective, encounters a range of humanity that includes troglodytes, Norse gods, and the ghost of poet Samuel Taylor Coleridge. In spite of his success as a novelist, Adams thinks of himself as a humor writer, but he is serious about environmental concerns: he has donated his talents to a number of charities and has cowritten a book called *Last Chance to See* about places and animals in Indonesia, Zaire, New Zealand, China, and Mauritius that are being destroyed by industrialization.

Plot Summary

Earth

As *The Hitchhiker's Guide to the Galaxy* opens, Arthur Dent wakes to discover bulldozers ready to tear his house down in order to build a freeway bypass. He goes out and lies in front of the bulldozers. The foreman cannot convince Arthur to move. The foreman insists that the plans have been on display for months and that Arthur could have filed a complaint if he wanted to, but Arthur says he knew nothing about the plans until the day before, and when he did learn of them, he found them "displayed" in a locked file cabinet in the dark basement of the local planning office.

Ford Prefect is a friend of Arthur's. Arthur doesn't realize that his friend is an alien who has been stranded on Earth for fifteen years. He is a researcher for *The Hitchhiker's Guide to the Galaxy*, a book explaining how to travel the galaxy on less than thirty Altairian dollars a day. Ford drops by Arthur's house and asks Arthur to join him for a drink. Ford manages to convince the foreman to take Arthur's place lying in the mud so that the house will not be torn down. Once in the bar, Ford explains to the disbelieving Arthur that the world is about to end.

Overhead, huge yellow spacecrafts are hovering, but no one on earth notices, except for

Ford Prefect. The ships are Vogon spacecrafts, and the Vogons announce to Earth that they are there to demolish the planet in order to build a hyperspatial express route, as stated in plans that have been on display in the local planning department on Alpha Centauri for fifty years. The Vogons destroy the earth.

The Heart of Gold-1

Meanwhile on the opposite spiral arm of the galaxy, Zaphod Beeblebrox, the two-headed President of the Imperial Galactic Government, is attending the unveiling of the *Heart of Gold* ship, a top-secret project that is only today being revealed to the public. Zaphod steals the ship, taking with him Trillian, a girl he recently picked up at a party on Earth.

Hitchhiking

Seconds before Earth is destroyed, Ford hitches a lift on one of the Vogon ships, taking Arthur with him. The Vogons hate hitchhikers, but luckily they employ the Dentrassis people as their caterers, and the Dentrassis love to annoy the Vogons, so they gladly picked up the hitchhikers and hid them in a small cabin in the ship. Ford explains this to Arthur, and hands him *The Hitchhiker's Guide to the Galaxy* so that he can learn more. He also puts a Babel fish in Arthur's ear. The fish allows Arthur to understand any language.

The Vogons discover Ford and Arthur. They torture the hitchhikers by reading them Vogon poetry. Then they throw them off the ship. According to *The Hitchhiker's Guide to the Galaxy*, it is possible to survive in deep space for thirty seconds if you hold your breath, but it is highly improbable that one will be picked up by another ship during those thirty seconds. Twenty-nine seconds after being thrown into deep space, Arthur and Ford are rescued.

The Heart of Gold-2

Arthur and Ford are picked up by the *Heart of Gold*, which is powered by the Infinite Improbability Drive. Once the ship is out of improbability drive, Trillian and Zaphod order a depressed robot named Marvin to fetch the hitchhikers and to bring them to the control cabin. Ford already knows Zaphod because they are cousins. Arthur already knows Zaphod and Trillian because he was at the party where Zaphod picked up Trillian, also an earthling, after Arthur had spent the whole night trying to talk to her.

They all retire to separate cabins to sleep and think about the day's events. In the middle of the night, however, they reconvene in the control cabin, where Zaphod reveals that he found the planet Magrathea.

Magrathea

Magrathea was once the home of an industry that built custom-designed planets for the very wealthy. When the wealthy ran out of money, Magrathea disappeared. Ford does not believe that it ever existed. As they approach the planet they hear an answering machine on the planet announce that Magrathea is temporarily closed for business. Subsequent recordings ask them to leave, and then inform them that two guided missiles are headed towards their ship. They attempt to evade the missiles, and finally Arthur turns on the improbability drive.

The ship continues on as though nothing has happened, except that its interior has been redesigned. The missiles have turned into a bowl of petunias and a whale, both of which fall to the planet below. The ship lands. Zaphod, Ford, Trillian, Arthur, and Marvin (the depressed robot) all exit the ship, Trillian pausing only briefly to bemoan the fact that the white mice she brought with her from earth have escaped. They find the planet barren and desolate, but the whale's impact has opened a crater into the surface, and Zaphod, Ford, and Trillian set off to explore this, leaving Arthur and Marvin on the surface.

While heading down the passageway Zaphod reports that he has discovered that his brains have been tampered with and that the person who did this left the initials "Z. B." burned into the synapses. Before he can say more, a door shuts behind them, and gas begins to pour into the chamber.

Meanwhile on the surface, Arthur encounters a

Magrathean named Slartibartfast, who takes Arthur to the factory floor of the planet and shows him that a new earth is being built. The original Earth, he explains, was actually an organic computer commissioned by mice, who ran the planet and used it to conduct experiments on men. Because Arthur looks confused he explains further. Long ago some very intelligent beings had designed a computer to figure out the answer to the big question of life, the universe, and everything. The computer took seven-and-a-half million years to conclude that the answer was forty-two. Unfortunately it was not able to come up with the precise question for which this was an answer. But it designed another computer that could find the question. That computer was Earth, and all the creatures living on it during its ten million-year program were part of the computer, except for the mice, who were the creatures running the computer. Unfortunately, the earth had been destroyed only minutes before it came up with the correct answer, and so the mice needed a new computer.

After Zaphod, Ford, and Trillian wake up and recover from the gas, they discuss Zaphod's brain. Zaphod believes that he altered his own brain, but he does not know why. A man enters and announces that the mice will see them now.

Arthur is also brought to see the mice. He finds his friends sitting at a table along with Trillian's mice. The mice inform him that they want his brain as they think it may have the question encoded in it. They have been asked to appear on a television show to reveal the question. Arthur and his friends try to escape, but the doorway is blocked by armed guards. Just then an alarm sounds and a voice warns that a hostile ship has just landed on the planet. In the confusion Arthur and his friends escape. The mice decide to make up a question.

The intruders, however, turn out to be cops after Zaphod. They fire on Zaphod and the others until suddenly their life support systems fail. Zaphod, Ford, Trillian and Arthur return to their ship, where they find Marvin, who explains that the cops' ship committed suicide when he talked to it. They leave Magrathea, and Ford suggests that they stop at the Restaurant at the End of the Universe for a bite.

Zaphod Beeblebrox

Zaphod is described as having two heads and three arms, the third arm having been attached "to improve his ski-boxing." As the President of the Imperial Galactic Government, Zaphod was presiding over a ceremony unveiling the *Heart of Gold*, which was the first ship to run on Infinite Improbability Drive, when, on impulse, he paralyzed all of the onlookers and stole the ship.

Zaphod is not sure what compels him to do the things he does. For most of the book he assumes that his freewheeling, happy-go-lucky personality drives him to seek danger and allows him to talk his way out of it. "And then whenever I stop to think— why did I want to do something?—how did I work out how to do it?—I get a very strong desire just to stop thinking about it." Thinking about this, he runs a brain scan on himself, to see if someone else has put ideas into his mind: after careful searching, he finds that his brain has been tampered with, and that the culprit signed his initials. They are his own initials, indicating that he was the one who altered his own brain, without knowing it. He is convinced that he had himself made President of the Galaxy just to steal the *Heart of Gold* and travel to Magrathea, but he does not have a clue as to why it was necessary to do that.

Arthur Dent

Arthur was born and raised on Earth, and he is the book's protagonist. When the novel begins, Arthur wakes up to find that bulldozers outside of his house in England are ready to demolish it so that a bypass for the expressway can be built. While he is trying to stop the demolition by lying in the way of the trucks, his friend Ford Prefect comes and convinces him to go to the pub with him. It turns out that a similar event is happening on a much larger scale—that the Vogon race is about the demolish the Earth in order to build a new by-pass —and that the beer that Arthur drank at the pub was necessary to prepare his muscles for space travel.

Arthur's main function in the novel is that of an observer. He is the one to ask questions, to bring out facts that the other characters are already familiar with. Throughout the novel, Arthur is referred to derogatorily as Earthman" and "Monkey Man," the latter because of humans' relationship to their ancestors, the primates.

Eddie

Eddie is the computer on board the *Heart of Gold*. He is as annoyingly cheerful as Marvin is depressed. As the ship plummets toward the surface of Magrathea, for example, the crew is terrified, but Eddie sings a happy song, interrupting itself frequently to tell them how many seconds there are until impact. Later, Zaphod programs it with an "emergency back-up personality," but that personality is whiny and argumentative.

Flook

One of the computer programmers who was responsible for programming Deep Thought, the second greatest computer in the Universe of Time and Space, to solve the ultimate question of life, the universe and everything.

Prostetnic Vogon Jeltz

The commander of the Vogon ship that provides Arthur and Ford an escape from the destruction of Earth. He first tortures the stowaways by reading his awful Vogon poetry to them, then orders them thrown out of the ship into space.

Loonquawl

One of the officials in charge of the ceremony on the Great and Hopefully Enlightening Day, when Deep Thought, after seven and a half million years of computation, is supposed to reveal the Answer.

Lunkwill

One of the two computer programmers who was responsible for programming Deep Thought, the second greatest computer in the Universe of Time and Space, to solve the ultimate question of life, the universe and everything.

Majikthise

The elder philosopher from Cruxwan University. At a ceremony when the computer is ready to give its answer to the question of life, the universe and everything, Vroomfondel and Majikthise are honored as "the Most Truly Interesting Pundits the Universe has ever known."

Marvin

A robot, referred to sometimes as the Paranoid Android, Marvin is a prototype of the Sirius Cybernetics Corporation's new Genuine People Personality feature: unfortunately, the personality he has been given is terminally depressed. He is capable of solving complicated problems when asked, but he is also inclined to complain when asked to do the simplest tasks.

Tricia McMillan

See Trillian

Media Adaptations

- *The Hitchhiker's Guide to the Galaxy*. Video-cassette. Six-episode British Broadcasting Corp. (BBC) Television series. BBC Video/CBS Fox, 1981.

- *The Hitchhiker's Guide to the Galaxy*. Audiocassette. Read by Stephen Moore. Ontario: Music for Pleasure Ltd., 1981.

- *The Restaurant at the End of the Universe*. Audiocassette. Read by Stephen Moore. Ontario: Music for Pleasure Ltd., 1983.

- *Life, the Universe and Everything*. Audiocassette. Read by Stephen Moore. Ontario: Music for Pleasure Ltd., 1984.

- *So Long, and Thanks for All the Fish*. Audiocassette. Read by Douglas Adams. Beverly Hills, CA: Dove Audio Books, 1992.

- *Mostly Harmless*. Audiocassette. Read by Douglas Adams. Beverly Hills, CA: Dove Audio Books, 1993.

- *The Hitchhiker's Guide to the Galaxy: The Complete Audio Books*. Set of four compact discs. Beverly Hills, CA: Dove Audio Books, 1998.

Benjy Mouse

The mice of planet Earth are revealed to actually be from the ancient race that commissioned the Magratheans to create the Earth. Slartibartfast explains: "They are merely a protrusion into our dimension of vastly hyperintelligent pandimensional beings." When they find out that Arthur Dent was born on the planet and lived there up until a few minutes before its destruction, they offer to buy his brain in order to read the information imprinted there.

Frankie Mouse

The mice of planet Earth are revealed to actually be from the ancient race that commissioned the Magratheans to create the Earth. When they find out that Arthur Dent was born on the planet and lived there up until a few minutes before its destruction, they offer to buy his brain in order to read the information imprinted there.

The Paranoid Android

See Marvin

Phouchg

One of the officials in charge of the ceremony on the Great and Hopefully Enlightening Day, when Deep Thought is supposed to reveal the Answer.

Ford Prefect

Ford is a researcher for *The Hitchhiker's Guide to the Galaxy*. For years, he traveled from planet to planet by begging free rides, but as the novel starts he has been stranded on Earth for fifteen years. On Earth, he assumed the name Ford Prefect, thinking that it would allow him to blend in (although his cousin, whom he knew in childhood, calls him "Ford" in a later chapter, an inconsistency that is not explained). His disguise on Earth, that of an out-of-work actor, has satisfied the curiosity of people who might otherwise wonder about him. Because he is mostly used to introduce the concept of space travel and of *The Hitchhiker's Guide to the Galaxy* to Arthur, Ford's role in the novel drops off sharply in the book's second half.

L. Prosser

Mr. Prosser is a descendent of Genghis Khan, although he does not know it. He is in charge of the demolition crew sent to destroy Arthur Dent's house.

Slartibartfast

Described as a very old man, Slartibartfast is a resident of Magrathea, the planet where other planets are created. He is a planet designer, specializing in coastlines. He won an award for his work on Norway on the original Earth, and he has designed Africa on the replacement Earth with fjords—"I happen to like them," he explains, "and I'm old-fashioned enough to think that they give a lovely baroque feel to a continent."

Trillian

Trillian is a girl that Zaphod Beeblebrox picked up at a party on Earth, while she was talking to Arthur Dent. She is introduced in the novel as being "slim, darkish, humanoid, with long waves of black hair, an odd little knob of a nose and ridiculously brown eyes." She travels with Zaphod and is with him when he steals the *Heart of Gold*. The odds against picking up Arthur and Ford floating in space as they did are the same as her phone number on Earth.

Vroomfondel

Vroomfondel is the younger philosopher from Cruxwan University. Vroomfondel and Majikthise are honored as "the Most Truly Interesting Pundits the Universe has ever known."

Themes

Absurdity

One of the guiding principles of *The Hitchhiker's Guide to the Galaxy* is that of absurdity, of things happening randomly without cause or meaning. This does not mean that the whole book is a series of events that occur in random order. Most of the extreme examples of meaninglessness, in fact, do have a cause—they are the products of the Infinite Improbability Drive on the *Starship Heart of Gold*. The fairly logical explanation of the Improbability Drive in Chapter 10 allows the novel to introduce its most fantastic oddities and coincidences.

For instance, the *Heart of Gold* picks up Arthur Dent and Ford Prefect when they are dangling in space because it is highly improbable it would happen. The same force makes Arthur's limbs dissolve and turns Ford into a penguin; it redecorates the bridge of the ship with mirrors and potted plants; and it causes a whale to materialize in the skies above Magrathea. All of these events are notable for being shockingly unpredictable. These elements of absurdity would not have nearly as much impact if they occurred in an atmosphere of total absurdity, but the novel highlights them by placing them alongside of a struggle for reason, which makes the lack of reason stand out.

Characters are constantly trying to explain the sense of their actions, ignoring the chaos around them.

This pattern is established in the opening chapter, with the demolition crew coming to take down Arthur Dent's house. While Mr. Prosser is convinced that Arthur was given a fair and sensible warning of the demolition, to Arthur the fact that the plans for destruction were "on display" in a locked filing cabinet in a disused lavatory in the darkened, stairless cellar of the planning office, behind a sign reading "Beware of the Leopard," represents an absurd form of "giving notice." Throughout the book, bureaucratic thinking struggles against the natural absurdity of the universe and often creates its own, even more frustrating, kind of absurdity.

Nature and Its Meaning

Rather than being a source of meaning, as is frequently assumed, humanity is presented in this book as a taker of meaning, acting out the roles that are assigned by the animals around us. This is most evident in the interactions with the laboratory mice: scientists believe that they are manipulating the mice's behaviors in order to learn more about nature, but the mice are actually manipulating the scientists' behaviors to learn more about humans. To these mice, the meaning of the Earth and its ten-million-year history comes down to one particular instant, when, at a pre-programmed date and time, Earth will produce the Question to the Answer.

To the dolphins, the second most intelligent species on the planet (ahead of humanity), human life is worth saving, but when humans misinterpret their warnings of the coming cataclysm—whistling and backward somersaults—for tricks, the dolphins get into the spaceship they have constructed and leave. Even the topography of Earth has a meaning that is vastly different than what is usually ascribed to it by humans. The fjords of Norway, for example, are not a result of glacial development, but they instead have the appearance that they do because they were designed by Slartibartfast, who happens to like making fjords and in fact won several design awards for his work. In this way, the novel tells its readers that all of the things in the natural world do have a particular meaning, just as the greatest thinkers are prone to speculate, but that humans would never to be able to determine these meanings with the limited information at hand.

Permanence

The book begins with what would ordinarily be considered the end of all that we know—the destruction of the Earth—but then it goes on to explain a broader context in which the Earth's existence played only a small part. The Earth came into existence because it was manufactured by the Magratheans, who would never have done it without being paid for the job. So its destruction, like the demolition of Arthur Dent's house or the crumpling of a piece of paper, is irrelevant to the people who have used it. With this perspective of

Earth, and the limitless varieties of life forms that Arthur Dent encounters in his travels, the fact that Earth's existence is not permanent is treated as insignificant.

Topics for Further Study

- Make up a work order for the Magratheans, explaining the kind of world you would like them to build. Be specific about the kinds of geographical features and animals you would like to see, and explain why.

- *The Hitchhiker's Guide to the Galaxy* summarizes the whole Earth with only two words: "mostly harmless." Write up an extended entry for a guidebook that will explain your town in detail to people from other planets.

- Write a poem that you think might have been written by Paula Nancy Millstone Jennings of Greenbridge, Essex, England, whose work is identified in the novel as the worst in the universe. Explain the elements of your poem that you think make it so terrifyingly awful.

- Suppose that the novel is right in saying that humans are not in control of Earth, but wrong in believing that either mice or dolphins are the most intelligent animals on the planet. Which animals do you think might actually be an intelligent species from another world, controlling human behavior wordlessly? Why do you think so?

Culture Clash

In a sense, this novel presents the entire universe as belonging to a different culture that citizens of Earth just do not understand. The non-Earth characters, from Vogsphere, Betelgeuse, and Magrathea, all seem to understand each other, even in cases where they have not been introduced to each other's culture before. For example, both Ford Prefect and Zaphod Beeblebrox believe the planet of Magrathea to be a myth, but soon after they arrive they accept it for what it is with little further conflict. Even Trillian, who was born on Earth but has been traveling the universe for roughly six months more than Arthur Dent, is unshaken by the strange occurrences that she observes.

There are several explanations for the different attitudes displayed. One is that Earth is an insular culture, unfamiliar with the other races existing throughout the universe, and so Earth people are more prone to be surprised by new circumstances and more awkward in their reactions. Another might be that the customs of Earth people are, in general, uptight, and look even more so when placed beside the carefree attitudes of the rest of the occupants of the universe. Strategically, it helps this work as a comedy to have Arthur Dent come from a repressive culture and to have his sensibilities and drive for order offended by the casualness of those he meets. This follows a comic tradition at least as old as Shakespeare that pits sophisticates against the good-natured people with simple common sense.

Style

Parody

The Hitchhiker's Guide to the Galaxy is a parody of traditional science fiction adventure stories. A parody is a work that takes the conventions and rules of one form and uses them for comic effect. It is distinguished from a satire in that satire usually tries to point out human folly and vices in order to reform them, while the subject of parody is the style of writing itself.

Traditional science fiction takes the reader, often through the adventures of a common person like Arthur Dent, into a world where the universal laws of physics as we know them have been stretched beyond current capacities. Space travel is often associated with science fiction because introducing beings from other planets allows writers to account for the fact that they are able to manipulate reality in ways that are currently unheard of; time travel is often an important element for the same reason. Most good science fiction uses the different physical rules it presents to explore constants in behavior, while most bad science fiction introduces bizarre elements for their own sake, just to show off the author's active imagination. This book derives its humor from reversing the usual results that readers have come to expect.

For example, readers might expect the Earth to be destroyed in a war, so its destruction is presented here as a result of petty bureaucracy; the President of the Galaxy is not a fearsome sovereign but a joy-riding party animal; traveling through space, which has been the goal of multi-billion-dollar government programs, is presented as hitchhiking; something usually as insignificant as bad poetry is one of the most terrifying weapons used in the book. Traditional science fiction stories expend much energy explaining how things work under the rules they have created: this story adds preposterous elements at will, and does not insult its readers' intelligence by pretending that they make sense.

Episodic Plot

The story that this book is based on was originally written as a 12-part radio series for the British Broadcasting System. Being presented in installments created certain requirements for its plot structure. The action had to reach a peak every so often, raising the curiosity of listeners who would not be able to simply turn the page to find out what would happen next. At the same time, the individual segments each had to tell an independent story, in case someone heard just one episode in the middle of it all.

When adapting the series to a novel, Douglas Adams rewrote the story so that it would not just read like a string of events but more like a story; still, signs of the original structure are not hard to find. Points of heightened interest, such as when Arthur and Ford are seemingly doomed to drift in space, or Zaphod Beeblebrox's teaser at the end of a chapter that foreshadows description of the most improbable planet that ever existed," show the original strategy meant to hold readers' interest for a week.

Also, instead of following one broad stretch, the plot follows several distinct, sequential arcs: the destruction of Earth; the theft of the *Heart of Gold;* the encounter with Prostetnic Vogon Jeltz; the rescue from space; the approach to Magrathea and escaping its attack; the encounter with Slartibartfast; and the explanation of the ancient race seeking the answer to the Ultimate Question. Any of these episodes could be skipped without doing sustained damage to one's understanding of the whole story.

Anthropomorphism

Anthropomorphism is the practice, common in literature, of giving human thoughts, motives and behavior patterns to non-human things, such as animals or inanimate objects. It is most evident here in the thoughts that are ascribed to animals. This does not apply to the mice, because it is explained that they are not really mice but humanoid aliens in disguise. Yet no such explanation is offered to explain why the dolphins would be able or willing to conceive of a warning about the Earth's impending doom, or why the sperm whale that materialized in the air would think of the extended monologue that runs through its mind in Chapter 18.

In addition, the book derives continuous humor from the human-like personalities of the chronically depressed robot, given the common human name Marvin, and from Eddie, the sickeningly cheerful computer that becomes whiny after Zaphod activates its "back-up personality." Science fiction stories often speculate that advanced civilizations will program computers to interact with humans on human terms, which would mean that they would display some sort of personality—as the book explains, Sirius Cybernetics Corporation had programmed Marvin with a Genuine People Personality. *The Hitchhiker's Guide* takes that assumption to an extreme by giving the machines undesirable personalities.

Compare & Contrast

- **1979:** Iranian leader Mohamed Reza Shah Pahlevi fled the country. Shiite Muslim leader Ayatollah Ruholla Khomeini, returning from fifteen years' exile, took *de facto* control of Iran. In November, workers at the American embassy were taken hostage by terrorists with state backing. Throughout the 444 days they were held, American morale dropped.

  Today: Having played a key role in

the 1991 international military action against Iran's neighbor Iraq, the United States government is less hesitant to become involved in international conflicts.

- **1979:** Disco, a musical trend popular in urban areas throughout the mid-seventies, was at its peak. Big hair, big collars, and platform shoes were popular across the country.
  Today: Because of the changing nature of fashion, today's trends are destined to look ridiculous to people twenty years from now.

- **1979:** Comedy was very popular: *Monty Python's Flying Circus*, a British show from the early 1970s, was finishing its first run on American television; the young unknowns who starred on *Saturday Night Live* were making movies; and comedians like Richard Pryor and Steve Martin were playing to capacity crowds at stadiums.
  Today: The proliferation of comedy shows on cable television and of franchised comedy clubs in malls have diluted the impact and popularity of comedy in America.

- **1979:** A partial meltdown at the Three Mile Island nuclear power plant in Harrisburg, Pennsylvania forced an evacuation of thousands of nearby residents and left Americans fearful of radiation poisoning from a larger catastrophe.

Today: The larger catastrophe that Americans feared in 1979 has not happened in the U.S., but some experts say that it becomes increasingly likely as the nation's nuclear power plants age.

Space Exploration

By the time *The Hitchhiker's Guide to the Galaxy* was published in 1979, many people had tired of the American and Soviet race for dominance in space. Twenty years earlier, there had been excitement and anticipation in the United States, spurred on by fear that the Soviet Union would be the first country to conquer space.

The first evidence of real progress in the exploration of space was witnessed in 1957, when the citizens of the world woke up one day to find that the Soviets had put an artificial satellite, *Sputnik I*, into orbit. In many parts of the world people could step outside and, looking into the sky, watch the satellite pass by. America, which was the only other country of comparable military might to the Soviet Union, entered into a competition meant to preserve national pride, as well as to prevent the Soviets from gaining superior missile technology.

Through the 1950s the lead in the space race shifted back and forth. The Russians put a living being, a dog, into space in 1957. The U. S. Congress established The National Aeronautics and Space Agency in 1958. The first human to go into space was a Russian, in 1961; the first American went into space the following month. During the 1960s, Russia fell behind and America progressed steadily. The race was finally won on July 20, 1969 when an American was the first human being to walk on the moon. After that, both countries continued to explore space, but public interest dropped off. *Apollo* missions landed on the surface of the moon five more times; the Soviets built a space station in 1971; an American space station, *Skylab*, was built in 1973.

Because the missions were generally successful, public interest dwindled until danger or irregularities occurred. In 1979, the most covered story in space exploration was that *Skylab* was due to fall out of orbit. Since nobody could accurately predict where it would land, the world anxiously watched forecasts for months—a far cry from the expectant days when new boundaries were being broken, new challenges being surpassed. When it did come down, it rained debris over western Australia and over the Indian Ocean, but no one was hurt by the falling wreckage.

The Internet

The basic concept of the Internet had started in 1969, when the Defense Department of the United States ordered that information that was crucial to national defense should not be held in one place where it could be vulnerable to a nuclear attack. In response to the order, the University of California at Los Angeles organized a "node," a network that could disperse information to decentralized locations. Soon, other universities linked their databases with UCLA's, as did government research facilities, so that by 1975 there were nearly 100 nodes with international connections.

At the same time, advances were being made that would bring personal computers into homes. By the 1970s, word processors using cathode ray tubes had become available, offering offices ways of handling the flow of written materials economically. In 1976, Wang Laboratories produced computers that could connect terminals within offices, while that same year Apple Computers was formed. In 1977 the Apple II personal computer became the first economically feasible computer for home use —it ran through the screen of the common television and backed up its memory on simple audio tape, but its $1300 price was much lower than anything seen up to then. In 1979, CompuServe Information Systems was launched, making on-line linkups available to people outside of the Defense Department/University system.

Critical Overview

Initially, reviewers praised *The Hitchhiker's Guide to the Galaxy*, pleased to have found a book that attempted to be humorous and was, for the most part, successful. "This hilarious and irrepressibly clever book is one of the best pieces of humor to be produced this year," applauded Rosemary Herbert in *Library Journal*.

Richard Brown, writing in *The Times Literary Supplement*, characterized Douglas Adams's writing as having "a posh-school, wide-eyed, naive manner related, perhaps, to the primitive manner currently in vogue in high-brow poetry circles." The main point of Brown's review, though, was to explore the relationship between the *Hitchhiker* books and the media, television and radio, that Adams was writing for when the books came into existence. Most reviewers categorized this book with science fiction novels and, in that context, found much to appreciate.

Because science fiction is a genre that often takes itself too seriously, critics have tended to take *The Hitchhiker's Guide to the Galaxy* and its sequels as a breath of fresh air. Lisa Tuttle, writing in the *Washington Post*, compared the book's relationship to traditional science fiction novels and concluded that "it's extremely funny—a rare and precious conjunction in a field where what usually passes as humor is a bad pun at the end of a dull story."

Like Tuttle, many reviewers saw this first book in the series as a reaction to the claustrophobic world of science fiction writing. Gerald Jonas, in *The New York Times Book Review*, pointed out that "[h]umorous science fiction novels have notoriously limited audiences; they tend to be full of 'in' jokes understandable only to those who read everything from Jules Verne to Harlan Ellison." Adams's novel, in contrast, was a "delightful exception." *Voice of Youth Advocates* reviewer M.K. Chelton felt that *The Hitchhiker's Guide* was "a bizarre, wildly funny, satiric novel," but did not feel that this made it an exception to mainstream science fiction, explaining that it had "lots of in-jokes SF fans will either love or loathe, and a free-floating irreverence which is irresistible."

As the series of books progressed and came to be known as *The Hitchhiker Trilogy* (even after the publication of the fourth and fifth novels), reviewers found it more and more resistible. They started tiring of the tricks that had won Adams their enthusiasm in the first place. John Clute, who reviewed *The Hitchhiker's Guide* for *The Magazine of Fantasy and Science Fiction*, acknowledged that the book was a joy. He also gave recognition to the less clever elements that it involved: "Given its music-hall premises, the tone of *Hitchhiker* is sometimes damagingly sophomoric, and there is a constant taint of collegiate wit in the naming of silly names and the descriptions of silly alcoholic beverages...." He went on to praise the novel as "one of the genre's rare genuinely funny books," but the elements that he pointed out tended to become more obvious to reviewers as they appeared in one book after the next.

Losing the element of surprise did not stop Adams from producing the series' fourth and fifth installments, and though reviewers, taking the series for granted, did not express further delight, there has been growing respect for Adams's growth as a novelist. While the first book in the series was appreciated for what it was not—a traditional science-fiction comedy—Adams's recent works have been praised for their characterization and plotting.

What Do I Read Next?

- This book is just the first in a series about Arthur Dent, Ford Prefect, and the colorful characters that they encounter in their travels through space and time. Fans have followed them through a series of five novels, including this one, *The Restaurant at the End of the Universe* (1980), *Life, the Universe, and Everything* (1982), *So Long and Thanks for All the Fish* (1984), and *Mostly Harmless* (1992).

- For fans who have trouble keeping a handle on the characters and events in the *Hitchhiker* books, Pocket Books published a guide in 1981 that covers the original trilogy, called *Don't Panic: The Official Hitchhiker's Guide to the Galaxy Companion*.

- Mark Leyner's novels have been compared to Adams's for their unpredictability and sense of fun. His most recent, 1997's *The Tetherballs of Bouganville*, bounces through a cultural land scape strewn with markers of our time, such as scholarship awards, lethal injection, screenplay writers, supermodels and videos.

- The fiction of Kurt Vonnegut has always been admired for its ability to present a comically unreal world in a slightly plausible way. One of his early books, *Cat's Cradle* (1963), is a darkly funny story about the end of the world.

- The standard for this type of story, in which a normal person is thrown into a surreal world of tortured logic, was set in 1865, by mathematician Lewis Carroll's fantasy *Alice's Adventures in Wonderland*.

- Douglas Adams's latest achievement is a collaboration with Terry Jones, a member of the Monty Python troupe, *Starship Titanic: A Novel*, published in 1998. Adams wrote the introduction; and the idea behind the book was his—Starship Titanic is first mentioned in *Life, The Universe and Everything*, one of the original *Hitchhiker's Guide* trilogy; and Adams wrote the interactive CD-ROM of the same name. Jones wrote the actual book.

Sources

Richard Brown, "Posh-School SF," *The Times Literary Supplement*, No. 4147, September 24, 1982, p. 1032.

M. K. Chelton, in *Voya*, Vol. 3, February, 1981.

John Clute, in *The Magazine of Fantasy and Science Fiction*, Vol. 62, No. 2, February, 1982, pp. 34-5.

Rosemary Herbert, in *Library Journal*, September 15, 1980.

Gerald Jonas, in *The New York Times Book Review*, January 25, 1981, pp. 24-5.

Lisa Tuttle, "As Other Worlds Turn," *Book World— The Washington Post*, November 23, 1980, p. 6.

For Further Study

Douglas Adams, *The Original Hitchhiker Radio Scripts*, edited by Geoffrey Perkins, Harmony Books, 1985.

> This book contains the scripts for the original radio show on which the novel was based; an introduction in which Adams talks about his writing; another introduction by the producer of the show, Geoffrey Perkins; and many notes about the script.

Brian W. Aldiss, introduction to *Hell's Cartographers: Some Personal Histories of Science Fiction Writers*, edited by Brian W. Aldiss and Harry Harrison, Weidenfeld and Nicolson, 1975, pp. 1-5.

> Aldiss discusses the effect that the dropping of the first atomic bomb on Hiroshima had on science fiction and science fiction writers.

Thomas M. Disch, *The Dreams Our Stuff Is Made of: How Science Fiction Conquered the World*, The Free Press, 1998.

> To understand how well *The Hitchhiker's Guide to the Galaxy* parodies the science fiction tradition, and how much it follows the rules that it lays out, it helps to understand

what that tradition is. Disch has
published in almost all genres, and
he is a cult figure in science fiction.

John Griffiths, *Three Tomorrows: American, British and Soviet Science Fiction*, Barnes and Noble Books, 1980.

Although this book gives little
consideration to the *Hitchhiker*
phenomenon, which was relatively
new when it was written, it is helpful
for those interested in considering
how the ideas of science fiction
differ on both sides of the globe.

David Leon Higdon, "'Into the vast unknown': Directions in the Post-Holocaust Novel" in *War and Peace: Perspectives in the Nuclear Age*, edited by Ulrich Goebel and Otto Nelson, Texas Tech UP, 1988, pp. 117-24.

Higdon traces developments in Post-
Holocaust fiction.

Carl R. Kropf, "Douglas Adams's 'Hitchhiker' Novels as Mock Science Fiction," *Science-Fiction Studies*, Vol. 15, No. 1, March 1988, pp. 61-70.

Kropf suggests that Adams's books
could be seen as Mock Science
Fiction, much as Alexander Pope's
The Dunciad is a mock epic.

Kurt Vonnegut, *The Sirens of Titan*, Dell Publishing, 1970.

A science fiction work which shares

many common plot devices and themes with *The Hitchhiker's Guide to the Galaxy*.

Lightning Source UK Ltd.
Milton Keynes UK
UKHW020030110123
415109UK00015B/1038